# SHOW ME THE WAY

## A GRIPPING TRUE STORY ABOUT TERROR ON THE LAKE AT MIDNIGHT.

## MERLIN JOHNSON

outskirts
press

Outskirts Press, Inc.
http://www.outskirtspress.com

Paperback ISBN: 978-1-4787-8032-8

PRINTED IN THE UNITED STATES OF AMERICA

# About the Author

After a short time at Phoenix College, Arizona, as a premed major and training as a student pilot, Merlin served on active duty in the US Air Force. He served at Luke AFB in Arizona and at Chanute AFB at Champaign/Urbana, Illinois, where he was trained in mechanical engineering and precision machine work. He attained a 4.0 grade average, top of his class, and was asked to stay on as an instructor.

He met and married Peggy Jean Keeling from Detroit, Michigan, and moved to Santa Rosa, California, and had his first job with Rudolf Wendel Inc. as a machinist, and learned Wendelighting at that firm. Then he moved on to Casella Lighting in San Francisco a large manufacturing firm making custom light fixtures and chandeliers of all types. About this time, he secured his California C-10 general electrical contractor's license and started his own business called Artistic Lighting and Electric in Marin County, California. He designed, developed, and manufactured a custom lighting framing projector for the lighting of paintings and fine art works and called it "Merlinlights." This unit made it possible to confine the light beam, with a sophisticated lens system, to the actual size of an object only.

When lighting paintings the light is focused on the canvas only, with no light on the frame or adjacent walls. His works have been featured in *Architectural Digest, Designers West*, and many other magazines. Their three sons are carrying on the family tradition of custom lighting: electrical installations, control systems, engineering, and "MerlinLight."

Our lighting installations can be found throughout the United States, Canada, and Japan, and in fine homes everywhere. Merlin started his business, (Artistic Lighting and Electric) in 1959 in the San Francisco Bay area and was one of the first Lighting Designers in that area specializing in the lighting of High End single family homes. We also opened an office in Palm Desert, Ca. to service the Palm Springs area, Los Angeles, Orange County and San Diego as we had many clients in those areas. Our clients were some of the country's best known and prominent business owners, Hollywood movie people and famous Industrialists. We enjoyed a full range of relationships with many wonderful people taking us from San Francisco to southern California and all points in between. We have lighting installations in Mexico and Canada and our most famous job was being selected to do a very large home and estate for Mr. Takahashi in Karuizawa Japan, who is a world leader in the manufacturer of miniature ball bearings, The Minibea Co. I made 13 trips to Japan to accomplish this task. It was a wonderful experience working with the Takashashi's, the Japanese designers, engineers and the Japanese people. It was the high light of my working years.

My next book will be based on the adventures and experiences of a forty seven year career in the lighting and electrical business.

Many of our installations can be found at www.merlinlights.com

Merlin Johnson

Merlin's "Words of Wisdom" that I have lived by these many years:

Move on! Nothing in the world can take the place of persistence.

Talent will not: nothing is more common than unsuccessful men with talent.

Genius will not: unrewarded genius is almost a proverb.

Education alone will not: the world is full of educated derelicts.

Wealth will not: the world is full of rich and unhappy people who are prone to dysfunctional personal relationships, addictions, and poor health.

Persistence, determination, faith, and hard work are omnipotent.

Seek, and you will find your destiny.

Ask and it shall be given to you.

And as Mark Twain once said:

Throw off the bow lines:

Sail away from the safe harbor:

Catch the trade winds in your sails:

Explore, Dream, Discover:

Merlin Johnson, with his wife and family, had many years of boating pleasures and experiences in the Pacific ocean at Newport Beach, San Diego Mission Bay,and Catalina Island California. Lake Havasu London Bridge Arizona, and Big Bear Lake and Clearlake in California which brings us to my following story, 'Show Me The Way'.

*To my wife PeggyJean, who has been my soul mate for all of these years, and to our three sons Duane, Glenn, and Eric and their families, who are carrying on the family traditions of Superior lighting and electrical installations, and for being of service to others wherever they may be!*

# Show Me the Way

This is a true story about a boating event that happened on Clear Lake in California on a holiday weekend, resulting in a terrible accident that caused the death of an individual and with serious injuries to others. The names have been changed to protect their privacy. The principals in this story are Jon, his wife Jenny, and their dear old friends Caitie and Matt.

It was one of those glorious days that we enjoyed so much at the lake with its wonderful weather and crisp clean air. I was up as usual around 5:00 AM. Barney, our Sheltie dog, was sleeping by my wife who likes to sleep in—and the dog too! I woke up Barney and said, "Come on, Barney, it is time for a walk." He reluctantly agreed and we proceeded outside.

The birds were singing loudly, and a slight breeze was filling the air with the scent of the lake, trees, and flowers. We walked down the street to the marina and turned back home. By this time Jenny was up and we had coffee and chatted.

I had recently purchased a twenty-four-foot Sea Ray Sundancer cruiser which was my second love, and we had it berthed at our local marina.

I said to Jenny that it was such a beautiful day, why don't we take the boat out for a cruise as we had nothing else planned, and I was always ready for a boat ride. She agreed and said, "Why don't we call Caitie and Matt and see if they would like to go with us?" as they lived close by. I called them and they were delighted and accepted the invitation. We discussed taking some food and drinks—enough to make a day of it. They met us some time later and we loaded the boat with the supplies. The ladies put things away in the cabin and Matt and I cast off the lines.

We proceeded out of the marina canal, which was narrow, curved, and wooded and always reminded me of the old movie *African Queen*, going down the river with Bogart and Hepburn, and we moved out into the lake, which is large. Clear Lake is the largest natural lake in California—only Lake Tahoe is larger—but about half of it is in Nevada. Clear Lake is roughly shaped like an hourglass, with Upper Lake being a large body of water to the north, and Lower Lake, somewhat smaller, to the south with a narrow connector in the middle. The lake is long—about twenty-six miles long and about six miles wide. From the narrows, another body of water goes east to Rattlesnake Island and to the Sulfur Bank areas. This narrows area can be very rough, with high waves when the winds come up with strong currents, and can be dangerous for boaters.

We cruised all around the lake and Caitie said that she wanted to go fishing, and we did but we did not catch anything. She was so wild with her casting out that she tossed her line out and over mine and we tangled.

She laughed loudly and said, "Hey, Jon, was that as good for you as it was for me?" I replied, "You Bet!" You never know what is going to come out of that pretty little face. Matt was embarrassed and Jenny did not like it!

As it was getting late now, I remarked, "Hey, let's go over to Rattlesnake Island and park and have dinner." Everyone was happy about that and we did. I drove around the island and finally found a sheltered cove and parked in the tules. I asked Matt to drop the anchor and I set it. By this time we were all hungry and thirsty and the ladies went below and started preparing some food. Matt and I had some wine and enjoyed some small talk. We ate our dinner and just sat there and enjoyed the most beautiful sunset that we had ever experienced as the sun settled over the mountains and over the water in glory. As it was now fully dark I said, "Why don't we just stay here for the night?" as the weather was perfect, no wind and calm, and everyone was delighted to do so. The sounds of the birds and wild animals on the uninhabited island were incredible as it got dark, as they were bedding down for the night as it was now about 10:00 PM.

The ladies were preparing our sleeping arrangements as Matt and I were spellbound with the display of stars in the black night sky and the wonderful warm evening weather.

It happens that Lake County enjoys the best air quality in California. There was no moon, nothing but darkness, and the lake was as black as ink. All you could see were small dots of light around the lake and shoreline and the faint outline of the mountains against the night sky.

About this time Chris and his wife Carly, with their young son Scott and along with Chris's cousin Justin and his friend Jim, had just finished a great dinner at Harbor Inn—a beautiful resort facility on the lake. On the way out they stopped at the fuel dock and topped off the two bulkhead tanks—one on the port side and one on the starboard side—with about thirty-five gallons each. They were driving a twenty-one-foot Ski Cruiser boat, which sits very low in the water. They started out to return to Lakeport—about a fifteen-mile slow drive to Upper Lake—around 10:30 PM but stopped in the narrows briefly. With motor running and navigation lights on, Chris and Jim had to relieve themselves while adrift. This is common for boat occupants as most small boats do not have toilet facilities.

These navigation lights. One on port side and one on starboard side indicate your presence in the water, and the masthead light on top shows whether you are moving forward or backward.

This lighting is for others to see you in the water, and they do not provide any light for sailing for you as the headlights do in your car.

For those who have not experienced night sailing, it is a unique experience in the dark. As mentioned previously, boats do not have headlights, and even if they did you could not see anything, as the light would just be reflected off the water unless there was something in the water. Consequently, you travel slowly and enjoy the starlit night sky and the dots of light around the shorelines. I always liked sailing at night, and about two months ago I installed two high-powered floodlights on the bow of the boat—not for sailing but for entering the marina in the dark and docking. I also had a CB radio on board as I did not have any radios or telephone facilities in those days.

It was now about 10:30 PM, and Jenny and Caitie were seeing to the sleeping arrangements below deck. Matt and I were seated on the aft deck talking and enjoying the night air, when a deep feeling of foreboding came over me for no reason and without warning!

I interrupted Matt in the middle of his conversation and said that we have to go back to the marina. He said, "WHAT, go back? What are you talking about, Jon?!" he said in disbelief.

I called down to Jenny and Caitie and said that we were leaving and to get things in order, and they were as shocked as Matt by my comments.

I had such a feeling of urgency come over me that I had never experienced before. I told Matt to pull the anchor on my command. I started the engine, released the anchor, and started backing out of the tules. He again shouted at me, "What are we doing now, Jon?" I replied that we were going back to the marina. Needless to say Caitie was very upset with me and so was my wife, who said, "What are we doing?" I was underway and heading out into the narrows. Caitie climbed out of the cabin and onto the foredeck and sat on the bow pulpit—a large mahogany plank that extends out over the bow—with her arms draped over the safety railings and shouting, "If we cannot stay overnight at the island, I want to go dancing at the Harbor Inn resort!" I said sorry, and to come back into the boat as it is not safe and is illegal to ride up there while underway.

She always did her own thing anyway and stayed there all the way back to our marina. By now I was wondering what was wrong with me!! We started our slow ride back to the marina in silence. Everyone was so upset with me by now that no one spoke all the way back—and justifiably so! But I proceeded on as something was driving me, I know not what.

As it was so quiet now, I had time to reflect on our longtime friendship with Caitie and Matt. Matt and I worked together before he and Caitie were married. Matt and I worked for two lighting and electrical companies in northern California and San Francisco, specializing in work in high-end single-family homes. We had many good times together, at work and socially. In fact, we talked and laughed a lot remembering about some of our experiences when we were parked at Rattlesnake Island.

One time we were working at a client's home on 17-Mile Drive in Pebble Beach, California, when Matt asked me if after work we could stop by a ladies' shop as he needed to purchase a birthday present for Caitie.

Matt said that Caitie wanted a yellow polka-dot bikini bathing suit. I said, "Sure, we will go to Carmel which is close by, as they have many fine shops." As it was the end of the day, we cleaned up and loaded our tools in the service truck and drove to Carmel.

We found a very fine ladies' apparel shop and went in. We were talking and joking and there were two elegant sales ladies watching us closely as we walked around, looking at us in disgust in our work clothes, and I am sure thinking that we were gay. Matt was all over the place looking for bathing suits and asked one of the ladies for help. She reluctantly pointed to the area without saying a word. Matt found one in the stack of bathing suits, and held it up to look at it and hollered to me across the store, "Hey, Jon, how do you like this one?" I said, "It looks great!"

One of the ladies, with her poker face, took the suit from Matt to ring it up and said to him, "Which one of you guys are going to wear this?"

I could not resist it and I said, "He is," laughing and pointing to Matt. He replied, "Jon, you should not have said that," but we both laughed all the way back. I teased him later, saying, "How did it fit you, Matt?" No response! Another time we were out boating with Matt and Caitie, and we were all getting hungry and decided to go to the Harbor Inn for lunch. This is a large facility on the lake with entertainment rooms, restaurants, pools, a large marina, etc. The place was packed with people on the large outdoor deck on the lake at the marina. Many were at tables and standing with their food and drinks, and the music was playing and some were dancing. As I approached the dock, I had to wait a while as it was crowded with boats. I finally got to the dock, but there were so many other boats and waves and the water was very choppy due to all the boat traffic that it was hard to dock. I tried to slip in sideways to no avail and again nose first, but it was not to be. As soon as I got close in, the currents would push my boat back out away from the dock.

I asked Matt to stand by with a line, and tried again to get close and for him to try to catch onto a dock cleat to pull us up. I moved out again and back in, but Caitie was not to be outdone. She again climbed out onto the front deck of my boat at the bow pulpit in her bikini to help. I told her to get back as it was dangerous. Of course she did not. She was trying to step onto the dock from the boat.

As I again got close enough, she stepped off the boat with one foot onto the dock and with the other foot on my boat—virtually doing the splits. Again the boat is moving out again as her legs got farther and farther apart, one on boat and one on dock. I could not believe that they could stretch that far for such a little lady; then she disappeared, and down she falls into the churning waters of the lake. I was so frightened at this point, as if the boat might move back in and crush her between the boat and dock. Everyone on the dock by now is watching her, and in seconds Caitie scrabbled up the dockside ladder dripping wet onto the dock, laughing loudly and flailing her arms about as she gets a standing ovation from all. Matt was embarrassed again by his wife, but that's Caitie and we love her.

But all of these thoughts were fading away now, as I could see the lights at the entrance to our marina. I entered the canal in silence except for the steady hum of the motor and into my slip and docked. Matt jumped off the boat without a word and went to the men's room. Caitie was talking loudly and wildly with Jenny, and both were very upset and angry with me. By now I was very upset with myself as well, and confused by my own behavior.

By this time, it was about 11 PM. I was feeling very strange myself, and in spite of all the commotion around me, I heard a very loud dull thud from far out in the lake. Needless to say my hearing leaves something to be desired, but I heard what sounded like a car crash from the road down an embankment, and I shouted for Caitie to be quiet and told her that I heard something.

She did not, and I put my hand around her neck and covered her mouth and said again, "*Be quiet!*" She replied that I was hurting her! I apologized and said that I had no right to do that, Caitie, "but I am trying to hear as I heard something?" In a moment there was complete silence on our boat, and then we all heard a faint woman's voice crying out, "Oh my God, oh my God help us, please help us," and she was sobbing. This little voice was coming from the narrows, as sound really carries over the water at night when all is silent. The skin on the back of my neck was crawling now, and Jenny's and Caitie's too as we all heard these cries in the night!

I called for Matt, who was still off the boat and about twenty yards away, and told him to hurry and get on the boat as we were going out again. He replied, "What the hell are we doing now, Jon?" I was so motivated at that point that I started the motor, cast off the lines, and started backing out, and Matt had to run to jump on the boat. We told him what happened and we were all very quiet now.

We could hear sounds from in back of us from the beaches, where we heard music and people laughing and partying. As we got farther out into the lake, now we heard again, "Help us, oh my God help us, hit-and-run, hit-and-run, hit-and-run." By now we were all sweating with skin crawling but couldn't see anything. It was deathly quiet now—no wind or waves, nothing in sight. No one was talking; in fact it was so quiet now that I turned off the motor, and we just drifted along as we were all very apprehensive about the unknown. Matt and I were facing forward, and Jenny and Caitie were looking backward and to the side. We could not hear anything or see anything as the lake was jet-black. Suddenly without warning, we saw the most brilliant falling star shoot out of the heavens from overhead from our right, arcing over us and coming down to our left as it looked like it was crashing into the water in the west. We all stood frozen in time for a moment by this spectacular show, and then Jenny shouted out, "I saw something in the water."

I started the motor again and turned left toward the falling-star path. We proceeded forward but saw nothing and heard nothing, and after a short while I shut the motor off again and drifted.

By this time I was really confused. What is going on with me? I asked myself in silence. Then out of the blackness we all heard a woman's voice again whimpering and repeating, "Help us, help us, please someone help us!" I started the motor again and moved forward slowly and turned on the bow floodlights. Several hundred feet before us, we saw a flickering red light on the water. I speeded up, and by now we were in the middle of the narrows. We saw something but knew not what as we were straining to see and hear. Then we approached a debris field of broken fiberglass fragments and other materials floating around in the water—all kinds of things—and the smell of gasoline! Then the voice again: "Save us, oh please save us." As I moved cautiously through the debris, we finally saw a damaged boat in the water with many people on board.

A woman was waving frantically at us! I shut off the motor as we drifted through the debris and asked the woman if there was anyone in the water. "I do not want to run over anyone." She looked around her boat and said no. I started up the motor and moved around her boat to assess the damage.

There was a large breakout about four feet long on the starboard-side bulkhead, and the gas tank was punctured. The break was almost down to the lake waterline, and the interior floor of the boat was taking in water, and gas was floating around on the surface as the water was ankle deep by now. It was a miracle that the boat did not sink with all five people aboard, as the damage was severe. Had the breakout been a few inches lower, the five people and the boat would have vanished into the dark waters of the narrows at midnight, perhaps never to be seen again.

The skipper, Chris, was in the driver's seat, paralyzed with his left arm and hand on the bulkhead and his right hand on the steering wheel, and he could not speak.

His head was bent over, and I thought that his neck might be broken. His wife Carly was seated on the right side, clutching her small son Scott between her legs and the only person who spoke through this ordeal, and they seemed uninjured.

They had two friends aboard seated in the back. One was Justin, who was shaking so bad and trying to light a cigarette! I literally screamed at him to stop before we all blew up, and he did!

The other man was Jim, who lay dead at Justin's feet on the floor of the boat and partially between Justin's legs, with his head in a grotesque position! The boat had several inches of water and gas in it on the floor. This horrible sight will live with all of us forever.

Due to the severity of their injuries, I chose to not try to move anyone to our boat but to leave them be in their boat and tow them in. I did not want to tow them in from behind, as I was afraid their boat would sink taking in more water.

I moved alongside and asked Matt to lash our two boats together, pulling up the right side to slow the water entry into their boat. Jenny, against my wishes, climbed into their boat and sat with Carly to console her and her son, and they prayed as we moved along silently. When he had them secured to our boat, I called in on my CB radio for help on channel nine. I did not have a marine radio or any telephone facilities on board. Fortunately, I had an almost immediate radio response from a man in Lower Lake who heard my distress call. I described our condition and asked him to call the police, fire department, and for ambulances, and for all of them to meet us at my marina and that we were about two miles out in the narrows and coming in. I started in at slow speed, and Matt watched closely to be sure they would not be swamped with water and sink as we were going in. This was very stressful for me as I wondered what we could do if they started to sink. As we moved along at very slow speed, my boat started overheating due to the extra load and not enough water circulating through my engine. I had to shift out of gear and speed up the motor every so often to keep my engine cool.

About ten minutes later, we heard a boat approaching us at high speed from the rear. It was two off-duty policemen who were attending a BBQ across the lake and who'd heard my distress call and were coming to assist us. I thanked them and said we were OK right now but to please stand by in case of trouble, and they followed us in closely.

This was the longest, most heart-wrenching two miles that I had ever driven or experienced. Imagine the terror that Carly and her son experienced sitting on a sinking boat in the middle of the lake at night, and Carly having the fortitude to cry out for help, for who knows how long, until she was about to lose her voice, and we heard her.

I now asked Carly what had happened. This is unbelievable but true. She replied that Chris and Jim were standing up and relieving themselves when they heard the roar of a boat at very high speed approaching them.

By the time they realized it was going to hit them, Chris pushed Carly and his son down under the dash, but he and Jim could not sit down in time fast enough and they were hit broadside violently. The boat climbed over Chris's boat and stalled, landing on top of them all.

A moment of silence and Carly heard a man say, "We hit something." The other man answered, "I think it is a boat" and "Let's get the hell out of here." With that they restarted the motor, backed off, and left these people at their mercy in the middle of the lake. Carly was shouting at them, "Hit-and-run, hit-and-run, hit-and-run," to no avail as they motored away as she sobbed!

As I finally approached the canal to our marina, we saw red lights coming down the road to the docks from everywhere—police cars, fire trucks, ambulances, etc. What a beautiful sight to behold. I pulled up to the gas pumps, and I spun both our boats around to put Chris's boat against the dock for access. Within minutes the emergency people were everywhere.

They secured Chris's boat and I detached mine. They took Carly and her son away first, then installed a plank behind Chris's body to protect his neck and ready him for transport. They took Justin away and removed Jim's body and laid it out on the deck with a plastic mask over his face and tested the body to prove that he was dead.

What a pitiful sight it was to see Chris, still immobile and paralyzed, clutching the wheel of his boat. Jenny and Caitie got off my boat at the fuel station and attended to Carly and Scott as best as they could as they loaded the ambulances.

Matt and I returned to my slip and docked the boat, and we were mentally and physically exhausted! We sat for a moment in silence, and then I said, "Matt, can you believe this day???" He just shook his head and said nothing. We then walked back to the fuel station to rejoin Jenny and Caitie. They loaded up the ambulances and they sped away. I heard a medic say that they did not think that Chris would make it. Carly and Scott were OK but in severe shock at this time when they told her that Jim was dead and she broke down.

Jenny and Caitie took Carly and Scott to the hospital, as they would not let her ride in the ambulance with Chris.

The police officers asked Matt and me to return to my boat for statements and depositions, which we did until almost 4:30 AM. One of the officers received a radio call from across the lake from the police department there and was told that they'd arrested two drunken fishermen who went into a bar and asked for drinks very late at night. The bartender was suspicious as both men looked injured, especially one of them. When he asked them what happened, one replied that they were fishing and hit something in the water, probably a log. The bartender called the local police and they were arrested. I was very happy that they were apprehended so quickly. Jenny and Caitie returned to us from the hospital, and we all went home and crashed into a very restless sleep. Later that morning when I got up, feeling groggy and mentally and physically exhausted, my mind started to wander.

Why did I get a premonition NOT to spend the night at Rattlesnake Island? Why did I hear calls and sounds from the woman with my poor hearing that others did not hear? Why did I have such a strong urge to go back to my dock? Why did a falling star lead us in the direction of the accident?

Why was the water in the narrows so calm that night? Had it not been, the boat would have surely been swamped with the waves and all five people would have disappeared in the black waters of the lake and been lost.

Several days later, after we returned home, we could not get this incident off of our minds and we were very concerned about the welfare of the survivors. I called the local hospitals around the lake, but they were not there. I called hospitals in Sonoma County and Marin County and finally found them at a hospital in the bay area. We located Chris at his hospital and called them to arrange for a visit. We checked in at the hospital and received his room number from the receptionist.

We proceeded to the elevator, and when we stepped out of the elevator on the upper floor we saw Carly and her son Scott coming out of Chris's room. When she saw us she got very emotional and ran to us with hugs and kisses and cried. She did not remember our names but immediately took us into Chris's room.

When Chris saw us, both he and Carly were sobbing as we approached his bed, and they thanked us over and over again for saving them that fateful night. Fortunately Chris did not have a broken neck but some other non-life-threatening injuries and was recovering well. He related to us that on the night of the accident, he heard a boat approaching at high speed and stood up to get a better look to see it.

He said that it was like the scene from the movie *Jaws* when the shark came up on the back of the boat. He saw the bottom of the boat that crashed into them had a tri-hull, as the bow was high out of the water due to high speed.

He pushed his wife and son down low but could not sit down fast enough to avoid the collision, and then all went black.

He told us that in his younger years he'd worked as a commercial fisherman serving on large ocean-going vessels. He said that the number-one fear of professional seamen was not drowning, which would be quick and somewhat painless, but having the boat catch fire and burning.

He said that immediately after the accident, "I was paralyzed and could not speak although I could hear." He prayed fervently in silence that Jim would not light a cigarette as he was a chain smoker, as the bilges were full of gasoline and if he did they would surely all burn up. He prayed that if this was to be, to all drown quickly and not to burn. We had a long and delightful visit with them and apparently he recovered, and they all returned home and we never heard from them again!

This incident will live with us forever and is a constant reminder that one's life can be snuffed out in an instant, and we must be thankful of it and live life to the fullest while we are still here. I can only conclude that the Lord "Showed me the Way" that tragic and fateful night of terror on the lake.

The End

Lightning Source UK Ltd.
Milton Keynes UK
UKOW05f2329030317

295864UK00014B/508/P